25-99

FAIRS & FESTIVALS

FAIRS & FESTIVALS

Uma Vasudev

wisdom
tree
ACADEMIC

By arrangement with
Department of Tourism, Ministry of Culture, Government of India

Published in 2007 by

wisdom
tree

Wisdom Tree
4779/23 Ansari Road, Darya Ganj, New Delhi-110002
Ph: 23247966/67/68

Text © Uma Vasudev

Photo credits: Amit Pasricha-cover; Amit Mehra-page 1,7,16,17,30,38-
39,46,54,56,63,66,67,70,73,74,84,86,96; Prem Kapoor-25,28,37,82,89,99; Phal Girota-
2,4,12,20,24,26,33,34,35,44,49,50,51,93,94; Hemant Mehta-22,77; Rajeev Thankur-59;
M Balan-81; K Guruswamy-102; Isha Yoga-6

ISBN   81-8328-074-9

Conceptualised and published by Shobit Arya for Wisdom Tree; *edited by* Manju Gupta; *designed
at* SN Graphix *and printed at* Print Perfect, New Delhi - 110064

Preface

In India, the landscape is primarily of celebration. Barely does one festival end to commemorate a season, when another follows to honour a God, a Prophet or a saint. And because the seasons vary in India – from the Himalayan snows in Kashmir and Himachal to the sun-baked days of the East, from the monsoon lashing and the rolling seas in the West to the flowering greens in the South, and the three iridescent colours of the waters of the Bay of Bengal, the Indian Ocean and the Arabian Sea converging at the triangular southernmost tip of Kanyakumari – the call for a festive commemoration is unending. Even death, if it comes at the ripe old age of 100, is celebrated with a band accompanying the commemorative chants to thank the gods for a life well lived.

The 29 States and six Union Territories that constitute the Indian Union have Hindi as the main language, English as the second, and 18 officially recognised regional languages, as listed in the Constitution, for each state where education is imparted up to the level of university. Otherwise there are 35 languages, each spoken by a million people. There are approximately 22,000 dialects forming the base for a tapestry of sound within which are woven India's folk songs and melodies, reverberating to a 5,000-year old past and lending themselves to experiments with modern jazz and fusion. Tribal rhythms merge with regional folk-dance forms to beat time to changing norms which continue to connect with a past in terms of classical norms defined by ancient treatises and incorporated in mythological lore. The inspiration for Indian classical dance remains *Shiva*, the Lord of Cosmic Dance and for sound, it is the *Nada Brahma*, the *Om*, which is the all-perfect enunciation for all melodies to flow.

The festivals of India become the face and voice of this ancient tradition, the variety and expression of the creativity of its people. It is in its festivals that the country finds its many faces, its innumerable forms, its kaleidoscopic colours, its innovative spirit and yet within that runs the defining commonality that says emphatically: this here, is India.

The 25 festivals in this book have been chosen with a view to pinpointing the divergence of traditions and customs which the many religions in India stipulate for celebration. What comes out of this cultural cauldron is the commonality that manages to let so many cultural, religious and racial differences not only live under that one roof called India, but find their own individual path to commemorate a racial, mythological or historical memory while celebrating a cultural continuity.

Writing about these festivals was for me like going through a whole process of civilisational memory and yet again experience the unique blend of cultural strands that weave the magic of this land. So many diversities, so many religions, so many colours, so many landscapes, so much of much-ness that can hold you perennially enthralled!

Uma Vasudev

Contents

Editor's Note

India, home to one of the most ancient civilisations, is a unique example of cultural and geographical diversities. Dissimilar cultural practices are deeply rooted in people's daily lives even in the 21st century. Indian history is the fruit of geography, and geography the root of history. The history of several millennia has merged with phenomenal geographical variations to create the incredible India of today.

India is incredible in its landscapes, and the people who adorn her. Its rituals and traditions; sculptures and paintings; dance, music and theatre; handicrafts, fairs and festivals; monuments and manuscripts; and its varied cuisine – each is a definite statement that only India can proudly pronounce.

Myriad streams and rivers have been flowing for centuries in their own special terrain, sometimes forceful, sometimes gentle. Despite all kinds of obstacles, they flow on. When these waters reach the ocean, they mingle, and become one huge ocean. Similarly, these diverse, astonishingly rich and colourful cultural currents create a harmonious hymn known as India, even as they retain their unique individual identity.

This series of Incredible India presents 10 books on different cultural aspects of the country, written by well-known experts on the subject. Uma Vasudev, a well-known writer has taken up 25 fairs and festivals out of hundreds of them celebrated all over India. They are basically connected with the cycles of seasons and human life. Some have religious content, some others have agricultural content and yet some others have social content. Some are celebrated all over India, some in language and community regions, and some in small tribal pockets.

Festivals give life and colour to life which otherwise could be monotonous and drab. As the author says, the festivals of India become the face and voice of ancient traditions. There is a saying in Oriya language, *'Baro masara tero parba',* which literally means there are 13 festivals in 12 months. This expression actually denotes the fact that there are more festivals than the number of days! The variety and expression of creativity of the people, big or small, rich or poor are manifested through dance, music, paintings and sculptures, special cuisine and costumes.

Tribal fairs in different parts of the country are a class apart. In this book, the author has briefly written only about the tribal fairs of Madhya Pradesh which has a large belt of tribal population.

The fairs and festivals selected for this book represent the rich fare spread all over the country and celebrated throughout the year. The festival is celebrated differently in different parts of the country. The bottom line is: 'Let's be together and enjoy together'.

Basant Panchami

It is so typical of the traditional Indian attitude that the concept of learning is associated with joy, rather than with a gravity that can make the entire process a case of hard labour. This attitude is epitomised in the festival of Basant Panchami, which, weather-wise, heralds the spring, 'the prime of all seasons'. Nature is at its ecstatic best, signifying the ripe time for the birth of the Hindu calendar. It is typical also in the use of symbolic interpretations that India resorts to with respect to worship of Saraswati, the Goddess of Learning, at a time when the season of spring is at its best. There is a lovely anecdote, albeit mythological, which alludes to the predicament of Brahma, the Creator, about how he should give both logical and aesthetic shape to the then chaotic world. That is when Saraswati, the voice of reason within him, said, "With knowledge." What can exemplify better and more creatively for a civilisation's reference point than this simple aphorism!

For added benefit in enlarging the concept and giving knowledge its full dimension, Goddess Saraswati is also the symbolic head of the arts: music, dance and literature. So it is in its totality that the universe was ordered. And it is in the affirmation of that totality that the festival of Basant is celebrated. *Basant* means 'spring' and *Panchami* signifies 'the time' — the fifth day of the waxing moon in the month of *Magh* (February) of the Hindu calendar. With spring in the air, the soil rich with the yellow mustard flowers swaying in the cool breeze, the sky above in rich contrasting blue and the people clothed in matching mustard yellow *sarees* and *kurtas* to vie with the flowers, Basant becomes a celebration of spring with spirits soaring

sky high. This is accompanied with kites flying, swaying and playing in competition in the sky spread to infinity above.

When celebrated in a fully traditional manner, the sky is so full of kites on the day of Basant that it looks as if an unknown species of birds is afloat in the heavens! But soon enough the kite flying turns into a competition. There is a flurry of activity up in the sky when one kite-flyer seeks to edge the other off his field by cutting the thread of his kite and as soon as the other's kite sinks down, you hear the cries of triumph, "*Bo kata!*" (I've got him)! So particular is the adherence to custom on that day that even the sweets that are for sale or served to friends and guests are tinged with yellow, the colour of spring! So popular is this festival that there are compositions even in classical music describing the event and even a *raga* or melody named after it. In fact, *Raga Basant* has been conceived in notes that signify the celebration of spring.

Basant has the same connotations in each state of India, but the emphasis changes in the way it is celebrated. In Bihar and Orissa, it is the agricultural aspect that acquires prominence with the worship of the plough and of the earth itself as the giving mother. In Bengal, the more intellectual side is revered, with Saraswati Puja and the objects of learning like books, pencils, and perhaps, these days, the computers, forming the modern idols.

Bihu

In India there is very little to choose from in the manner in which a religious festival is held and the one that celebrates Nature's bounty. The real basic difference lies only in terms of attendance at places of worship. Everything seems to become an excuse for celebration, or for a ritual ceremony. And as the climatic variations extend from the snows in Kashmir and Himachal Pradesh to the lush green meadows of Kerala and Assam, the sand dunes and landscape of Rajasthan, from the undulating hills and meadows of Madhya Pradesh to the rich environs of Tripura and Manipur in the north-east, the festivals too take on the hues and symbolic modes of each region.

Most of these festivals centre around either the spring or the harvesting season. There is however no festival anywhere which celebrates the season of winter and snow. Even in Kashmir or Himachal, Christmas would be more of a private affair among the Christian community, but not a celebration of Nature as such.

In Assam, there is this one festival, the Bihu, which does spread over spring and autumn and even on to winter. It is normally held in mid-April. Understandably, the significance of the Bihu celebration gets muted as it goes on from the autumn to the winter season!

Spring is where the heart is, for the Indian. And if spring comes, the first showers cannot be far behind in an area which thrives on the beneficence of the clouds. With the onset of New Year, the people feel thrice blessed. So the celebrations are in triple accord and are mixed with local legends to explain the whimsicalities of Nature. For instance, the winds that sweep the land and bring with them the first

welcome showers are allied in public lore to the story of a woman called Bardoichita who, it is said, brings the rain with her when she comes to visit her mother!

The Bohag Bihu is celebrated in April and for a community dependent on its agricultural base, the instant obeisance is to the cow, the milk-giving source and mainstay of the agricultural community. In fact, so venerated is the cow that the first day of Bohag Bihu is reserved to commemorate the species. There is a whole ceremonial ritual which begins with washing of the cow's feet, rubbing it with oil and then sending it off happily with garlands round its neck. Sometimes the cows are even taken to the ponds and rivers for a bath and then fed *pitha,* a brand of local cake. The children particularly participate in a big way.

Typically, however, of the Indian sensibility which still prevails, no festival is ever complete without paying obeisance to the very people who have brought you into being — your elders. And typically, therefore, the second day of this festival is reserved to receive blessings from the older generation. It is called Manuh Bihu. Not only do the young bow before the elders comprising mothers, fathers, aunts and uncles but the younger women weave the *gamochas* or *bihuwan* on the family loom to gift it to their elders and friends.

The most colourful aspect of Bihu celebration is the performance of songs and dances by the young. This comprises almost a separate category of celebration. The young girls wear *kopon,* a local orchid, in their hair. They clothe themselves in the traditional costume called *muga kapor* and decorate themselves with local ornaments, like *kerumoni, gamkharu* and others. The men, not to be left behind, wear their traditional attire and dance to an orchestra of local instruments like the *dhol,* a drum, a flute made of buffalo horn called *pepa* and the *gogona* — a wind instrument culled out of bamboo. Modernisation unfortunately has entailed a shift of venue when necessary — from the clean open air to the confines of a stage in a hall.

LEFT
Abandon in the colours of spring

Buddha Purnima

The day the Prince from the Sakya tribe of Nepal was born, the moon came out in full glory. Siddhartha Gautama, son of King Shuddodana and Queen Mahamaya, was born in the year 566 BC in Kalpataru, now called Lumbini. The story goes that the pregnant queen was on the way to her mother's house, when she had to stop in the gardens of Lumbini to give birth to the child. The moon was at its zenith, and the heavens sent down a rain of flowers. This made the little baby jump up and take seven steps. From each of these spots then sprang a lotus flower which came to be associated with the Buddha. The event was to change the world and certainly the tenor of this royal line. For 29 years the young prince basked in the glory of his royal privileges, the love of his beautiful wife, Princess Yashodhara, and their adorable young son, Rahul. But one day, he saw the world of pain outside his privileged environs and felt the shock of realisation.

So he left his comfort, love and luxury to seek the true meaning of life. He found it after six years of meditation under the Bodhi tree and the town named after it, Bodh Gaya in Bihar. He was then only 35, but ready to impart his vision of enlightenment. So was born the Buddha or Siddhartha Gautama, with a vision that was going to capture half the world, this side of the east, from India to China, Japan, Mongolia, Tibet. Here then was no imperial army or arbitrary rule enforcing a change of religion or imposing a philosophical text. Here then was a complete message of love and realisation of the ultimate truth, and here too, was a methodology, which abjured the ritual in favour of the meditative, that is, the choice of the eight-fold path: the right view, thought, speech, action, livelihood, effort, mindfulness and contemplation, with recourse to wisdom, morality and meditation. Coming as this did in a caste-ridden society that obtained in India then, the Buddha's message of rationality as against blind faith and prejudice was like manna from heaven.

As a spiritual leader his message travelled far across half the world, from Syria and Egypt to Sri Lanka and the Far East, from Korea to Afghanistan and Khotan in Central Asia, such that he came to be called 'the Light of Asia' by Edwin Arnold, the famous scholar. To top it all, however, the Buddha is still considered part of the Hindu pantheon, as the ninth *avatar* of Vishnu.

Buddha, as Siddhartha, was born on a full-moon night. He attained enlightenment also on a full-moon night. And yet again, it was a full-moon night when he died and attained *nirvana*, at the age of 80 after he had completed the *sahasra chandra darshana* — one who has seen a thousand moons.

So the Buddha Purnima day, or night, is thrice blessed. It is in this month of *Vaishakha*, or April/May, that devotees offer their salutations to the Bodh or banyan tree under which the young devotee attained spiritual revelation. Those devotees, who wish, can visit Bodh Gaya in Bihar which has now become an international centre. There is a chanting of prayers by Buddhist monks in the monasteries or private homes, offerings of milk and scented water to the roots of the Bodhi tree, a circle of earthen lamps to light it up, and flags and garlands to adorn it. At Sarnath, where Buddha delivered his first sermon, a congregation of monks from India and elsewhere gather to offer their homage through religious chants and prayers. Celebrations are conducted and Buddhist chants are recited in monasteries built in commemoration by Buddhist countries like Burma, China, Tibet, Japan, Thailand and Bhutan. The architecture is unique to each country, but the reverberation of chants is a thread that binds all together.

PAGES 16 & 17
Buddhist monks — a resonance of prayers

Though the Buddha himself abjured any ceremonial ritual and propagated the belief that it is the path of self-purification which can enable one to attain *nirvana*, or the release from the cycle of rebirth, the Indians as a race just cannot stop from giving a ceremonial garb to any event! In fact, when two or three centuries after the Buddha's death, the two schools of Hinayana and Mahayana Buddhism came into being, the Mahayana section deified the Buddha, the Sakyamuni, into a deity. The statues of Buddha sprang up everywhere and here too the obeisance on Buddha Purnima takes the form of offerings of sweets, flowers and garlands to celebrate the divinity with a circle of lights. The chanting from Buddhist scriptures seems to spell an invitation to eternal bliss.

Christmas

Like Navroze of the Parsis and the two Eids of the Muslims, Christmas too owes its origins for the Christians in India to far off lands. But like the other festivals, Christmas too has acquired its own special Indian flavour in the manner of its celebration. Added to this is the regional colour. Christmas celebrated in Delhi is staid compared to the festive variations you find in Goa. And then there are the languages, the music and the variety of drums, which impart their own very special inputs! Carols, the songs in chorus, heralding the birth of Jesus Christ, are sung not only in the familiar English versions, but also in translations into many of the Indian languages. What is of singular coincidence is that Christ too was born, like Krishna, at midnight. He was born in a stable but Krishna, the Blue God, in a prison! Both the celebrations commemorate the special midnight hour, preceded and followed by festivities. While Lord Krishna's date of birth lies in a timeless era, the birth of Christ, the son of God as he came to be regarded, goes back to 4,000 years.

But the celebrations of the event began only in AD 98. The form that they took was derived primarily from the way the early Mesopotamians celebrated their New Year — with song, merriment, processions, carnival floats, particularly the carol singers who would go from house to house and enjoy the entire saga of feasts, including the exchange of gifts.

The miracle of the birth of Jesus was foretold in Israel, then governed by King Herod. A poor carpenter, Joseph, living in Nazareth was told by Mary, who had yet to become his wife, that an angel had visited her in a dream. He had said that she

would become a mother to Jesus, the Son of God. Soon enough, the miracle began to happen. Meanwhile Emperor Caesar Augustus decreed that all his subjects must go to their place of birth so that their names could be registered for a new tax. Joseph set off with the pregnant Mary for Bethlehem. On reaching there, they found accommodation only in a stable with hay to sleep on and it was there that their child Jesus was born. To herald the miracle, a big star appeared in the sky. The star was seen as far away as the east by Caspar, the King of Tarsus, Melchior and the King of Ethiopia, Balthazar. They constituted the Magi — those who know the science of the stars — and they realised the significance of the star in Bethlehem. So they journeyed over deserts and mountains and came laden with gifts to pay homage and on their return spread the word about the miracle.

Christ himself hailed from the Asian region. When Christianity came to India, it was clothed in the Western garb and spread mostly with the onset of British rule in India. There were the early Syrian Christians and there is a belief that evidence points to the presence of Christ in Kashmir. But basically, Christianity spread over larger territories when Emperor Constantine ascended the throne of Turkey and turned his whole empire towards Christian belief. With the spread of Christianity in the West, it became difficult for the followers to believe that this was an Asian religion in origin and that Jesus Christ was Asian and brown. In fact, if you see the early paintings magnificently displayed in the museum in St. Petersburg in Russia, Christ is painted everywhere as a dark complexioned figure. As the religion travelled westwards, so it seems did the complexion of Christ take on the hue of its newer devotees.

But despite the early attempt to keep celebrations of Christ's birth on a low devotional key, the original Mesopotamian traditions merged with the late Roman to characterise Christmas with fires, carnivals, exchange of gifts, candlelight decorations, prayers, yes, but also feasting and revelry, with some

LEFT
The thousand lights of belief

part taken also from the Roman festival 'Jo Saturnalia'! The midnight Christmas mass unites every Christian in a solemn affirmation of faith.

Christmas without Santa Claus would not be the occasion that it is, especially for children. The origin of Santa Claus goes back to his real identity as a man called Nicholas who lived in Myra, in old Turkey. He was jailed by Emperor Constantine's predecessor, Diocletian, who punished him for believing in Christ. He was released when Constantine ascended the throne. Nicholas became a bishop and it is believed that he went about doing the rounds of the town to do as much good as he could to alleviate individual suffering and thus gradually acquired the aura of a magical figure like Santa Claus.

In India, though everyone joins in with their Christian friends to celebrate the spirit of Christmas, which is also a national holiday, in Goa, it has its own magic. Ruled by the Portuguese, Goa became a Catholic stronghold, but the celebrations remained as local as can be with elephant processions, drums, umbrellas, dancing and singing with gusto, the city and its people revelling in its own traditional, exuberant spirit.

ABOVE
Santa Claus — the
spirit of joy

Diwali

Diwali is perhaps the most irresistible of the festivals of India. Though religious in connotation, it is secular in demonstration. The *puja* for the propitiation of Goddess Lakshmi, the Divine Progenitor of Wealth, and that too, in female form, takes place in the privacy of homes, as the primary ritual. Outside, it is all revelry, a festive decoration with *deepavali,* a string of lights, which illumine homes, buildings, anywhere and everywhere that the little earthen *divas,* filled with oil and brightly lit wicks, can be placed, appearing like twinkling stars on earth.

The celebration is to mark the joyousness which filled the populace when Lord Rama returned from 14 years of exile. It is the story of an ideal son who went on to become the ideal king in Hindu lore. Rama willingly sacrificed his succession in favour of his step-brother, Bharat, whose mother, Kaikeyi, had been given word by King Dashrath that he would fulfil her one wish which he had promised when she saved his life in his battle with the demons. On the point of winning the battle against the *asuras,* the nail, which held a wheel of his chariot, fell off. The volatile Kaikeyi who had insisted on accompanying him, immediately thrust her little finger into the *dhuri* or axle of the wheel to keep it going for Dashrath's winning encounter. On seeing her bleeding hand after his victory, Dashrath realised what she had done, and promised her a boon. Kaikeyi let it remain in abeyance. It was when Dashrath was going to relinquish the throne in favour of his eldest son Rama, that Kaikeyi reminded him of his promise. Dashrath, in his joy and gratitude, had said, "Not one, you can ask for two boons."

The wily Kaikeyi, the favourite queen of Dashrath, then dared him to the challenge. One, he should send Rama to exile for 14 years, and two, their son, Bharat, must ascend the throne in his place. Dashrath, honour-bound but heartbroken, thereby had to accede to her wish. Not only is this a story of the ideal king, the story of an ideal son, but also the story of an ideal brother. Rama went off to exile, accompanied by his wife Sita and another loyal brother, Lakshman. But Bharat, angry with his mother yet honour-bound to fulfil her wish, placed Rama's sandals on the throne, ruled the kingdom, but only in his brother's name till he returned.

Diwali celebrates Lord Rama's return to Ayodhya. It celebrates Sita's loyalty in braving the travails of exile; it celebrates a brother, Lakshman's resoluteness to stand by Rama in the many crises they had to face in those 14 years; and it celebrates the loyalty of Bharat who had to abide by his mother's oath but did it in a manner that he stands in mythological lore as the ideal brother, who disdained to rule but kept it on hold for his brother.

There was much therefore to rejoice in Ayodhya on the return of Rama, Lakshman and Sita. There were, first, the preparations. Everything had to glimmer, shine and be new. In preparation for the lights that would glow in every corner of the house, it had to have a shine of its own. So it had to be cleaned and painted afresh. In anticipation of the celebratory feasting that would follow, a symbolic new utensil is also bought on Dhanteras, a festival that falls three days before Diwali. And in anticipation, new clothes — everything is new — symbolising the auspicious beginning of Lord Rama's reign are worn by one and all. Like the myriad lights, the fireworks, and the

ABOVE
Goddess Lakshmi and Ganesh — auspicious beginnings

RIGHT
Spreading the light — women lighting diyas

mouth-watering dishes described in Valmiki's *Ramayana* which marked the celebration of Rama's return, so too does Diwali signify every year, for those who follow its traditions, hope, riches, merriment and almost an unending celebratory mood in which old enmities are forgiven and new bonds established. As it comes in the month of *Ashvin*, or October-November, even the weather in India is conducive to celebration!

ABOVE
The joy of togetherness

Durga Puja

Amongst the most ancient of Hindu religious texts, the *Puranas* are the oldest. They are the founts from which have sprung the beliefs, the rituals, the mythology and the symbolic reference points for discriminating between the good and the bad. The time span reads like the history of eternity.

And it is in the *Puranas* that you get the story of the birth of Goddess Durga as the triumphant symbol of victory over evil. There are no reservations here about the nature of the fight, no sermons about the methodology used to conquer what is bad, and no inhibitions about the manner of celebration, which entails equal participation of men and women. In fact, when the object of veneration, awe and power is a female deity, there can obviously be no social discrimination against the feminine order. Interestingly though, there is another aspect to the creation of Durga — that she was born from the power of the male, from the gods Shiva and Vishnu. The story, again as told in the *Puranas*, describes how the *asura* (demon) named Mahishasura became so powerful during the 100 years of battling the gods in heaven that he pushed them out and himself ascended God Indra's throne. That is when Shiva and Vishnu began to radiate a powerful light and as it grew brighter and brighter, it assumed the form of the all-powerful Goddess Durga — radiant, but fearsome, clothed in garments of silk and adorned with jewels, her thousand arms outstretched, spanning the universe in all directions, astride her special mount, the tiger, to bring the fearsome *asura* to his feet. This then is Durga in the form of the Mahishasuramardini, the destroyer of the demon-king, with the head of a buffalo.

Interestingly, the demon would assume the form of the *mahisha,* the buffalo, when he would go on a rampage to harass the gods. So it is the body with its head in the form a buffalo with which Goddess Durga engaged in a fearsome battle — a battle which raged over seas, mountains, creating volcanic eruptions and tremors on earth, till the defiant *asura* writhed with agony under her feet, still assuming different shapes to escape from the final thrust of her sword – signifying the victory over evil.

Goddess Durga thus represents power, but the power of good over evil and with no reservations about the necessary violence that the victory entailed. In fact, the celebration of Durga Puja entailed the sacrificial offering of the buffalo, as a symbol of the defeated *asura.* This is mentioned in the ancient treatises, like the *Skanda Purana* which says that if Goddess Harasiddhi, another name for Durga, is worshipped with the offerings of buffaloes on Mahanavami, the celebratory day of her victory, then all the wishes of her devotees get fulfilled. In fact, the principle seems to be that the greater the sacrifice, the greater the reward, as it says in the 7th-8th-century treatise, the *Kalika Purana*, with reference particularly to customs of sacrifice as they developed in Assam.

It was in the 11th century that the practice of animal sacrifice began to be curtailed, particularly in Gujarat where the then king preferred to follow the tenets of the Jain religion, which abjured all violence.

In 21st-century India, Durga Puja sees its most celebratory face in Bengal, though it is observed all over the country. Durga is worshipped as the symbol of power, as Mahishasuramardini, but the festivities include the deification of other manifestations of the goddess, as Lakshmi, the Goddess of Wealth and as Saraswati, the Goddess of Knowledge. The celebrations begin on the 7th, 8th and 9th days of the new moon in the month of *Asvani* (September-October). Of all the regions in India, where the festivities are held in veneration by the monarchical class for whom Durga was the war-goddess, it is now Bengal which literally goes berserk

LEFT
*The worship of
Goddess Durga*

with the celebrations. Though the Brahmins still dominate the conducting of *pujas,* the musicians, the drummers, the *shehnai* players, are not only non-Brahmins, but even Muslims. In fact, in all the festivities connected with the scale at which open spaces are converted for stage performances, get-togethers and festivities, and in the bounty with which each individual home becomes host to guests, the question of caste and religious differences also seems to be offered as sacrifice at the altar of this goddess! On the 10th day, the festivities reach the penultimate frenzy when crowds wherever they are, follow the image of Goddess Durga to the rivers and the ocean, and give her back to eternity. These immersion ceremonies then resound to chants that fill the air and the hearts of the people with a frenzy of devotion.

In Gujarat, the Garbha and the Dandiya dances are performed by men and women in traditional costumes, indulging almost in a frenzy of rhythm, beating time in circular movements with sticks, and invoking the goddess with celebratory songs.

In all the classical forms of Indian dance, like Bharatanatyam, Kathak and others, the item about Goddess Durga's killing of Mahishasura is one of the most popular ones. It is enacted with particular empathy by the female dancers as a triumph of woman power, and not just that of good over evil.

LEFT
Durga of the many powers — on the way to holy immersion

Dussehra

Dussehra is perhaps one festival which is celebrated in many ways in every corner of India, but with a singularly intense passion in commemorating the triumph of good over evil. The good is represented by Lord Rama, the human face of Vishnu who is the Preserver, amongst the powerful Trinity of gods — the other two being Brahma, the Creator and Shiva, the Destroyer. Together they form a cyclic pattern of life, death and eternity for the Hindu religious consciousness. But Rama, as a human, is the ideal king of Ayodhya, the territory which has come to acquire therefore a sentimental significance for the believer. Dussehra is the festival which marks Rama's victory over Ravana, the king of Lanka, and what could be termed in contemporary lingo as the first *crime passionel*. The great King Ravana, a devotee of Shiva, became so learned a scholar, and so profound in his achievement that he began to pose a threat to the gods themselves. Also to use current jargon, he got too big for his boots!

Struck by her infinite charm and beauty, Ravana abducted Sita when she was in exile with Rama and Lakshman, only to realise that he had unleashed a historic storm which could destroy him or the other. Taken to war by the avenging Rama, it destroyed him, his brother Kumbhakarana, who slept though the blaze that engulfed Ravana's capital, and his son, Meghnath, who fought hard by the side of his father. There are stories within stories, full of symbolic meanings to suggest that this was no symbolic war. In the southern states in India, in fact, Ravana is worshipped as one of the great savants of learning. Dussehra celebrates his defeat as a symbolic one.

So, on Dussehra day, preparations begin in central parks of towns and cities and village squares, where three huge effigies of Ravana, Kumbhakarana and Meghnath seem to reach out towards the sky and are set

ablaze in the evening as a penultimate celebration to the tune of thundering cries of triumph by the crowds. It is only somewhere at the back of the mind of all, that burning the effigies still cannot burn away the regret that a scholar so great, and a devotee of the great Shiva to boot, should have let his ambition reach such megalomaniac proportions! But what the celebration of Dussehra does is to make people think in terms of what is good and what is evil in a form which is so participatory that on this occasion too, though it is primarily a Hindu festival, Dussehra almost demands participation by all.

Also, the various forms the Dussehra festival takes vary almost from state to state. In Bengal, the first nine days constitute the Navaratri, the time to be spent in worship. The 10th day celebrates the triumph of good over evil in the form of Goddess Durga as Shakti, the symbol of power and cosmic energy. She vanquishes the demon Mahishasura in a penultimate victory of good over evil. How the festive aspects intermingle with one another in the various states of India becomes evident in the final immersion ceremony of the idols of Goddess Durga riding a lion, like the idols of Ganesha, who are also set to vanish in the timeless antiquity of the waters — into the Arabian Sea in Mumbai during Ganesh Chaturthi and into the Bay of Bengal on the eastern side! One significant detail conveys how careful the ancestral heritage was and how it is followed to this day. It is mandatory for the idol-makers to carve their idols only from elements that come from the river or sea, so that the regenerative cycle is maintained!

Down south, the celebrations take in all the three aspects — wealth or prosperity, learning and power. They worship Goddess Lakshmi for bounty, Goddess Saraswati for learning and the arts and Shakti or Durga, as symbols of power. The 10th day is celebrated as Vijayadashami. This commemorates the value of education and the arts. Gujarat celebrates this with its famous Garbha dance.

But perhaps the most grand spectacle is seen in Mysore. Here, the magnificently draped elephants form a procession which parades through the town on the day of Dussehra and draws almost the whole populace into its orbit. Late in the evenings, when people walk away from the grand spectacle, the fire and the fireworks, the crumbling effigies and the raucous cries, there is the beginning of that quiet questioning within, urging one to discover more of what is right and what is wrong — that is actually what Dussehra is all about.

Eid-ul-Fitr

Of the two major Islamic festivals, the Eid-ul-Fitr and the Eid-ul-Zuha, it is Eid-ul-Fitr with which people associate the celebratory aspect. It comes at the end of Ramzan on sighting of the new moon on the first of *Shawwal*, the 12th month of the Islamic calendar. Because this is a lunar calendar, the exact date varies from year to year. The one month of fasting termed Ramzan or Ramdan, was enjoined by Prophet Mohammed as a disciplinary ritual. This implies fasting for the whole day and observance of strict austerity and abstinence from any pleasurable activity. For one whole month, then, not only do those who follow the tenets strictly fast for the entire day, they do not even drink water. Prayer five times a day, which in any case is the Islamic ritual, is followed even more strictly than usual. It is only the men however who go to the mosque every morning, before which they are given the mandatory dates to eat as part of the cultural heritage from Arabia, the region where Islam was born. The women stay back to pray at home. The evening meal therefore also remains frugal.

It is natural then that when the new moon is sighted in *Shawwal* at the end of this month of rigid frugality, there is a burst of enthusiasm. Though the intimation about the new moon comes from official sources, from the call of the religious leader or Mullah at the mosque (these days from radio and television), there were times when the sighting of the moon would become an excuse for young girls and boys to go up to the roofs of their houses to sight not only the moon in the sky, but the girl whom the boys constitute to be the moon in their lives, the *chand sa mukhra* — one as

beautiful as the moon itself! What follows afterwards is a round of feasting and revelry, primarily exchange of greetings and get-togethers over the speciality of the day, the *seyvian ki kheer* — a preparation of milk, vermicelli and sugar — which is served to whoever comes visiting throughout the day. That is why sometimes the Eid-ul-Fitr is also called *Meethi Eid,* the Sweet Eid or even *Seyvian ki Eid! Fitr* is supposed to be a derivative of *fatar,* meaning 'break' from *fitrat,* which means 'Nature', hence symbolising the bounty of God in bestowing all the benefits of Nature to man. Another connotation is that *fitrah* means 'alms', so here is an occasion which should spell the spirit of not only revelry at the end of a month of physical penance, but also the spirit of giving. It is mandatory therefore for Muslims that on this day they should give money in the form of 2½ seers (about 2 kg) of wheat as alms to whomsoever it can go to. The other stipulation is that on this thanksgiving occasion, as part of the obligation to society as a whole, they must also

ABOVE
The embrace that ensures togetherness

donate 2½ per cent of the value of their savings in the year in terms of jewellery, land, and personal wealth; that is, after deducting from any debts that they might have accrued. Under the Islamic law, a person is not allowed in strict terms to take any benefit from money deposited in the bank in the form of interest. In fact, one stipulation for those who wish to go on a pilgrimage to Mecca, the ultimate destination for the believer, is that the expenses entailed must come from direct savings and not from those bolstered by interest rates! Equality is the theme song of Islam. As the poet says:

> *Ek hi saf mein khade ho gaye*
> *Mahmud-o-ayaz,*
> *na hi koi banda raha na koi*
> *banda nawaz.*

> (In one line stand the poor
> with the king,
> here then is no difference between
> the ruler and the ruled.)

On Eid-ul-Fitr, everyone wears new clothes: the women don colourful, newly given or newly bought ones and the men wear white *kurta* and pyjamas. The children delight in their new finery and get *idi*, cash money, to spend the way they want. The older women cook the *seviyan ka kheer* early morning and it is mandatory for the men to taste it before they go to the mosque and the Eid lunch which relatives, friends and neighbours are invited to have. The young girls get busy having their hands decorated in exquisite designs which are drawn on their hands and feet with henna in the most intricate of patterns. Eid-ul-Fitr, like the Hindu festival of Diwali, becomes an occasion for friends from every community or from far off areas to come together in the sharing of joy.

PAGES 38 & 39
In prayer there is no difference between the ruler and the ruled — the Jama Masjid

Eid-ul-Zuha

Eid-ul-Zuha is another name for the more familiar Bakr-Eid, the sacrifice of the lamb or Eid-e-Qurban, the Eid of Sacrifice or Eid-ul-Adha. This Eid falls on the fixed date of 10th of *Zil-haj*, the last month of the Islamic lunar calendar. So unlike on the occasion of Eid-ul-Zuha, the sighting of the moon does not involve any celebratory excitement. In fact, it commemorates a very serious and grave, yet an exalting experience for the true believer. It revolves round the most ultimate of tests that a Divine force can stipulate to test not only the devotion but the inner strength of those who follow the faith! Nearly 4,000 years ago, Prophet Ibrahim proved to be one such man. He was called upon by Allah Taala, as the supreme Godhead is referred to by the Muslims, to sacrifice what he held to be dearest to him to prove that his faith in the Divine injunction was unquestioning. Hazrat Ibrahim, as he is referred to with honour, loved his son, Ismail, the most. So he decided to sacrifice him at Mina, adjoining Mecca. But being a father, the thought of seeing himself applying the sword to his own son's throat was unbearable. So before lifting the axe, as his son bent his head before him in filial obedience, the faithful Ibrahim wrapped his eyes with a cloth so that he would not see the inhuman act that he was to commit. He struck the sword. But when he removed the cloth and opened his eyes, he found, to his utter amazement, that instead of his son, it was a ram, which lay slaughtered. He realised then that Allah had put him to a supreme test and that he had passed it with such honour that it became the occasion for celebrations in the same mode.

On Eid-ul-Zuha, therefore, it becomes mandatory for a Muslim family to sacrifice a ram, a goat, even a camel, to commemorate this instance of blind faith and obedience to Allah's mandate. In strict terms the occasion calls for a sacrifice of one animal per member of a family. That is now the domain of the really affluent. Gradually this custom has come down to the sacrificial ritual being centred round one animal per family. Special prayers precede and follow this ritual act, which can be performed on any of the three days from the 10th to the 13th of *Zil-haj*. The meat has to be distributed in three parts in a mandatory ritual as part of Islam's continuing emphasis on the concept of equality. One part is distributed in the name of God or Allah, which means for the poor and the needy, another for neighbours and relatives and the third for the family. The distribution has to be so just that even each organ of the animal's body has to be divided into three equal parts!

Eid-ul-Zuha coincides with the time of the performance of Haj, the sacred pilgrimage to Mecca which is the centre of Islam. The Haj is performed two days before Eid, so those who are lucky enough to qualify for undertaking the pilgrimage look forward to celebrating Prophet Ibrahim's test of ultimate devotion in the holy city of Mecca itself. But the rules that govern those who can undertake the Haj are strict and if they conform to these rules, then it becomes mandatory for every Muslim to go to Mecca at least once in a lifetime. But, and this too is mandatory, he or she must be sound financially and physically, should have paid off all his or her debts and should be free of responsibilities. Those who can perform Haj during their lifetime are considered lucky and earn the honoured appellation of 'Haji'.

Ganesh Chaturthi

There is a mythological basis for the worship of Ganesha, the elephant-headed God, in India. It cuts across all regional and language boundaries and unites the followers of Hinduism in a ceremonial bond. It draws its source from the *Shiva Purana* legend based on the divine couple — Parvati, holding her many identities within her role as the supreme consort of Shiva in his manifestation as Shankar. The incident is innocuous; the result momentous.

The story goes that Parvati, in order to have her bath in privacy, created an idol out of her own body, breathed life into it, and set it up outside with strict instructions not to let anyone in. When the great God, Shankar himself, came striding up to their abode in the Himalayas, the obedient idol refused to let him in. Furious that his will should have been flouted thus, Shankar cut off the idol's head. There was an absolute crises. Parvati wailed and shouted: "That was my son, carved out of my own body, and therefore your son, too." The great Shankar was so desirous to make amends that he told Gan, his servant, to go immediately and bring him the head of the first creature that he would see. Gan rushed off, saw an elephant, immediately cut off its head and presented it to Shankar, who then joined it to the idol's body and brought it back to life, albeit in howsoever different a form. Hence, in the Hindu pantheon, the birth of the elephant-god! Shankar then proceeded to make further amends — he termed his son *Gan*, meaning 'army', and *ish* or Lord; hence Ganesh, the Lord of the Army.

Ganesha, however, is also worshipped as the God of Auspicious Beginnings. This belief emanates again from an incident when all the gods went to pay homage to

Lord Shiva and Parvati at the Himalayan peak. They were offered *modak* made of divine nectar. Their two sons, Ganesha and his brother Kartikeya, also wanted to have the *modak*. But there was only one. "Whoever circles the Earth fastest will get the *modak*," the Divine parents challenged them. Kartikeya set off promptly, but Ganesha took a circle round his parents, touched their feet and sat down. When Kartikeya came back, he was told that he was the loser as Ganesha had understood that the whole world was contained in their father and the mother. So the *modak* went to Ganesha. It is then that Shiva gave him the blessing that was to make the elephant-god a household deity. "Before any new undertaking, it is your image that the people will seek for blessing." The result: Ganesha is not only a temple God; he is in every home and every office where people hold to this faith. He is in that sense transcendental.

Though Ganesha as *vighna harta,* the Remover of all Obstacles, holds a special place in every Hindu's heart, his popularity in the state of Maharashtra knows no limits. The reason is largely political. The great Maratha warrior Shivaji, in his battle against the Mughals, sought to unify mass sentiment through a common platform of culture and nationalist fervour. He started the Ganesha festival which took the form of a massive show of Indian solidarity against an invading enemy. After Shivaji's death, this mass involvement petered out till it came to another period in India's history — the fight against the British. In 1894, the British banned public assemblies. The great nationalist, Bal Gangadhar Tilak, took a leaf from Shivaji's example, and turned the celebrations of the Ganesha Mahaotsav (festival) into an occasion for a collective affirmation of India's identity. That is when the idol of Ganesha seemed to pour out of the skin of every inhabitant — from the private *puja* corners to public, ceremonial installations, a gathering of worshipful force to reveal to the enemy a united face. Since then, the Ganesha Mahotsav has become, sentimentally, the most uniting force of any religious occasion, particularly in its home in Mumbai.

LEFT
Ganesha, the idol of auspicious beginnings

The celebrations have to be seen to be believed. They begin on Ganapati or Ganesha's birthday after days of preparation, when his statues are installed not only in temples and public places, but in sanctified corners of every Hindu home. The largest apparently is installed, 30 ft high, in Khairatabad in Hyderabad. But it is Mumbai which sees this celebratory occasion at its peak after a continuous course of singing, chanting, drum beating, on the 10th day, when the moon is seen in its full effulgent glory. This is the day when the idols of Ganesha are immersed in the great ocean lapping the shores of this city; when the lights, candles, drums, chariots and people carrying the images ready themselves for the immersion ceremony. The idols are swept away or immersed into the water to a nostalgic chant rising above and over the waves in a sonorous, nostalgic refrain in Marathi:

Ganpati bappa morya
mangal moorti moray.

(Come back again, O Ganpati father!
Come back again, O auspicious one!)

The idols sway and dip and ride on the waves into the distance as the chants too sink in a sea of nostalgia.

LEFT
From eternity to eternity — from the hearts of the people to the heart of the ocean, to return yet again

Guru Parv

Simar simar simar
sukh payo.
Kaal kalesh tan
mahe mitayo.
Simro jaas bisumber ek
naam japat agnat anek.

(Chant the name of God. Chant his name forever.
Thus will you gain happiness. Thus may you be relieved of pain.)

The sound of voices in chorus in the early dawn, singing the lyrics in praise of Guru Nanak, led by a band of devotees, comes echoing down the streets, in a rise and fall of notes, and each person, if he or she is a Sikh, joins in. The crowd swells as it goes past each house. The people come out, donate sweet, milk, fruit, nuts, almonds, anything that they wish in a show of solidarity, irrespective of the religious belief that they might hold. The occasion is the birthday of Guru Nanak, the founder of the Sikh religion and who is said to have exclaimed at the moment of enlightenment, "There is no Hindu and no Muslim."

This became particularly relevant in India at a period when the rulers in India were Muslims and the majority of the population was Hindu. Guru Nanak himself was born in Punjab as a Hindu in AD 1469 in the house of Bedis or those who know

the *Vedas*. But it was on the issue of the abrogation of the division of Hindu society along caste prejudices that the Sikh tenets of equality found increasing support. In fact, it was at the time during the period of the 10th Guru Govind Singh in the 17th century that the Sikhs acquired the reputation of a warrior race. So strong was the bond between the Hindus and the Sikhs against the arbitrariness of Muslim rule in that period that it became a near norm for Hindu families to make their first son a Sikh! In fact, it is as a warrior race that a Sikh was enjoined to wear, symbolically, the five k's — *kesh*, a beard and long hair with the mandatory *kanga* or comb to keep it clean and a turban — there being no time to shave in the battlefield; a *kara*, a steel bangle with a cutting edge, symbolic of a weapon; along with

ABOVE
Into the hearts of the people the Guru Granth Sahib *in procession*

a *kirpan*, the long sword; the *kachcha,* the utilitarian long shorts — all time-saving devices for a battling soldier but which came to acquire over the centuries the signature of a religious order.

Guru Nanak simplified the Hindu code to its minimum by establishing the norms of a new order. The religious book, the *Guru Granth Sahib*, in which he set out his beliefs became the object of obeisance instead of the gods of the Hindu pantheon. He preached the brotherhood of humanity and the conviction that there is only one God. He accepted the Hindu belief in *samskara* and *karma,* the logic of the reward for good deeds and punishment for the bad in previous and ongoing re-births. But basically, what is celebrated on the birthday of Guru Nanak is the *Guru Granth Sahib* as the epitome of religious belief, with congregations thronging the *gurudwaras* where readings from the sacred text are conducted non-stop, or even in homes where a family holds a *paath* or religious readings for a more private participation.

The *Akhand Path* as it is called, lasts for three days in which the *Granth Sahib* is recited continuously without a break. There are also the *kirtans,* the devotional compositions, which form a significant aspect of the religious repertoire and have been set to classical *ragas* based on the Indian music system. Publicly, the *prabhat pheris* or the early morning processions, yield on the final day to a procession in which the *Guru Granth Sahib* is taken on a float decorated with flowers, throughout the city. It is led in front by five *kirpan*-wielding men representing the five main disciples of Guru Nanak. They carry the Sikh flag called *nishan sahibs* and are followed at the back by local bands and a swelling crowd of eager devotees. Booths are set up at vantage points along major roads, to offer passersby delectable cups of milk preparations, which invariably everyone takes as homage to the birthday of one of the most revered figures in Indian religious lore. In the evening, the *gurudwaras* and Sikh homes are lit with candles or *diyas,* or in tune with the times, with coloured electric bulbs.

PAGES 50 & 51
Young devotees at the Guru Parv celebration

Holi

Holi is the festival of colour. It is true that when the colours of green, blue, yellow, violet, pink and blue shower fall on you at the hands of an exuberant group of friends and relations who want to see you in rainbow hues, it becomes difficult to distinguish one victim from another, one friend from another, or even one enemy from the other. But it is the least of the intentions of this festival to damn you to anonymity. Perhaps that is the point. Such is the spirit that the enemy has to become a friend.

Holi celebrates the warm vibes of spring turning to summer. And, it is a celebration of freedom. You are no longer hemmed in by the cold and the desire to warm yourself indoors near an old-fashioned fireplace or rely on central-heating artifices. If you wake up early, you might hear a lone, joyful cry, "It ... is.... Holi ....Holi *hai-i-i-i*......!" But by 10:00 in the morning, there are hordes out on the streets, spilling out of houses, riding atop trucks, crowded into cars to visit friends with faces made anonymous through colour, creating the magic of camaraderie by drawing even strangers into their orbit of celebration. "Holi *hai*, Holi *hai*," they scream, laugh and shout and it is only the stuffy who can take umbrage. There is so much spontaneity and abandon in celebrating Holi that it becomes a cathartic experience. It spells freedom in the air.

And at places the scales of justice are evened out!

In village Barsana, in Rajasthan, for instance, Holi cuts across the sexual divide and like everywhere else, the male-female interaction is spontaneous. But here the

ABOVE
*At Barsana —
asserting feminine
power*

women are enjoined to take vengeance for all the years of sufferance at the hands of the male. They not only smear their men-folk with colour but chase them in a circle of dance, lashing at them with their broomsticks or *jharoos!* And the men have to take it in a show of submission! All the while, no matter what the context, there are special songs of Holi with sexual innuendos galore sung in teasing rhythms. These enchanting folk tunes have even been inducted into the Indian classical musical repertoire. There is one such which has been composed by the eminent exponent of what is known as the Rampur-Sahswan style by the late Ustad Mushtaq Hussain Khan and which he used to sing with matching allure:

Maarat more nainan mein pichkari
daiyan main to aise khilari se haari.
Garho rang lage chattiyan par,
khari lage pichkari.
Javo balam mora ajura phatak hai
tum jeete, hum haari, balamva.

(Oh, see how he sprays my face
with coloured water
no, no, how can I be game
for such play!
My breasts hang heavy,
drenched in hues
that shoot out from his
spray gun
and even cause my blouse
to rip apart
but happily do I concede defeat, my love
to this game of joyful colours!)

Traditionally, the celebration of Holi is centred round Lord Krishna and the *gopis,* the lovelorn maidens, who are basically a romantic guise for the devoted worshippers — the emotional and highly charged believers of the *Bhakti* cult. In singular terms, Meera, the princess who forsakes all for the love of God Krishna, stands as the supreme example of this unthinking devotion. Radha is the questioning one, through whom the ultimate union with the Divine is depicted in more equal, earthy terms.

Though Holi, a festival of irresistible bonhomie and camaraderie, has acquired quite secular tones, its origin can be traced to Hindu mythological lore. It signifies yet again, the triumph of good over evil in the form of a

story centring round a demon king, Hiranyakashyap and how he joined issue with the most invincible of the Hindu gods, Vishnu, the Creator. Fired by the ambition to be all-powerful, he did penance for which he obtained the boon of invincibility, to be able to project himself as the all-supreme object of worship. But his own son, Prahlad, a devotee of Vishnu, refused to accept this condition. The furious father ordered his sister Holika, who had obtained a boon for invincibility to fire, to sit with Prahlad on a burning pyre and let him go up in flames. But because of Prahlad's devotion to Lord Vishnu, it happened the other way round. Holika got burnt to death and Prahlad became forever the symbol of a true devotee.

The precursor to the joyful celebration of Holi is lighting the symbolic pyre on the eve of the festival to celebrate the destruction of evil epitomised by Holika — bonfire, crackers, a sense of triumph, and then the revelry. Contemporary celebration is moulded more after the Krishna-*gopis*-Radha legend. Here Vishnu, reincarnated as the young prankster Krishna in the city of Dwarka, uses the occasion of Holi to give a joyful turn to the male-female equation through the playful Krishna — the easy compatibility that it brings to the celebration of joy by cutting across the sexual divide and making the ancient, historical and mythological past appear as contemporary as can be. After all, it is 'H-o-l-i….*hai*!'

LEFT
Holi *hai!* Holi *hai!*

Janmashtami

According to some historians, Lord Krishna, believed by Hindus to be the ninth incarnation of God Vishnu, was a factual presence in the years 3200-3100 BC. Apart from his myriad roles through which he projects the essentialities of Hindu philosophy, he stands in the feminine consciousness also as the human face of the Divine lover. Krishna, beloved of the *gopis*; Krishna, Radha's passionate idol; Krishna, the consort of Rukmini; Krishna, the young prankster who has only to open his mouth wide for his mother to see that he holds the entire universe within his grasp; and Krishna who uses the great war of the *Mahabharata* to spell out to Arjun, the inspiring dynamism, the relentless logic, the philosophical brilliance of his exposition of the *Bhagwad Gita* on as unlikely an occasion as the great war between the brothers, the Kauravas and the Pandavas. This is where the question of life and death, right and wrong, the essential values get debated in what is considered to be an incomparable dissertation on the value of living and the inevitability of doing what is right, what must be done. They say that there is not a single plot of dramatic significance, on love, hate, passion and philosophy, all combined anywhere in the world which cannot be found in the myriad plots of the *Mahabharata*. And there, it is Lord Krishna who epitomises the philosophical direction.

Like Jesus Christ, Lord Krishna was also born at midnight, and whose birth is now celebrated as Janamashtami. Like most religious thought, the true meaning is embroiled in parables, in symbolic events, in the inevitability of the triumph of good over evil. When evil dominated through kings, emperors and criminals or, in those

days, dictatorships and democracy, the good took form in different ways to destroy evil. It was apparently the cry of Mother Earth, desperate to be saved from the atrocities of Kansa, king of Mathura, that set off a course of events of which is made the stuff of legend and mythology, wrapped either in the mantle of history or the opposite. Kansa, cruel and barbaric, was frightened by a prophecy that the 8th child of his sister Devaki and her husband Vasudev, would be responsible for his nemesis. So he put Devaki and Vasudev in jail and systematically got six of their progeny killed. It was when Vasudev held the 8th child in his arms that the prison gates opened, with instructions from God Vishnu himself to carry the child to Gokul and exchange his son for the daughter of Nanda and bring her back. When Kansa tried to kill this 8th child, she was transformed into Goddess Yogmaya and escaped his clutches. Eventually, of course, Krishna destroyed Kansa and re-established the dynasty of good.

Lord Krishna is embedded in people's mind in three ways — as the cowherd Krishna in Gokul, whose carefree, frolicking ways with the *gopis*, or the lovelorn maidens actually epitomise the *Bhakti Ras,* demanding the unquestioning devotion of the believer; as the passionate lover of Radha with whom he forms a partnership that stands as an example of perfect love; as the king of Mathura when he leaves all his past behind; and, as the philosopher God whose enunciation of the principles of belief, behaviour and ethics which form the *Bhagwad Gita*, place the war of *Mahabharata*, the conflict of love and devotion with the demands of what is right and necessary, in a perspective that remains open to intellectual debate.

Devotion, love, admiration for Krishna, the cowherd, the flute-player, the lover, the king, the philosopher charioteer, the author of the *Bhagwad Gita* — all this is rolled into the day of his birth. The first day of celebration commemorates his birth on the 8th day of a lunar fortnight in August. This is known as Gokulashtami. The second day is termed Kalastami or Janmashtami. It is on this day that celebrations take the form of a triangular

PAGE 59
Lord Krishna and the gopis — a partnership of love

formation of boys standing on each other's shoulders, reaching up to a 20-or even 40-foot pyramid to break a pot full of milk and curd and jostling for a taste of Krishna's favourite dishes! Some prize money is also distributed to those who reach the top by thus emulating the young Krishna's antics.

From frolic, fun and games, to amorous dalliance, to love for Radha as an example of an undying relationship, to king-philosopher and theorist, Krishna remains the most beloved of the gods.

Khwaja Chisti Urs

The first priority of a Muslim tourist visiting India or even foreign dignitaries of the same faith is to express a desire to pay homage at the famed *dargah* or resting place of Khwaja Moin-uddin Chisti. It is located in Ajmer in the north-eastern state of Rajasthan. Every year, the *dargah* at the saint's death anniversary, becomes the venue for thousands of men, women and children to congregate and pay homage to his memory. This annual Urs, as it is called, also becomes an occasion for people, after paying their obeisance to his memory, to tie the lucky threads round the pillars as a symbol of their faith that thereby their wishes will be granted!

Over the years, in typical Indian fashion, where even a Muslim saint is involved, the religious passion passes on to the Hindu majority, particularly on occasions like commemorating a saint like Khwaja Moin-uddin Chisti or Hazrat Nizamuddin Aulia whose shrine in Delhi also arouses a common religious fervour and international participation. It is an amazing sight therefore to see the community with its recognisably different religious stamp jostling together in ardent enthusiasm to reach the tombstone covered by a glimmering cloth and laden with flowers.

One feature which has come to be associated with the ceremonial tradition in both the cases is the music of the *qawwali* singers, a form of presentation which describes the attributes of Allah in dramatic, repetitive phrases taken up in chorus or in individual elaboration leading to, sometimes, a frenzied emphasis. Sometimes, the singers, other times, the audience, are swept into a trance. This tradition of the *qawwali* singing which is now a regular feature of the Urs at Ajmer and Nizamuddin

actually came into being first with Hazrat Nizamuddin's *dargah*. Nizamuddin was born in 1238 and died in 1324, but it was his great devotee and poet, Amir Khusro, who introduced in the *qawwali* — a mix of Persian and Hindi, making it a popular mode of singing for the commoner and the Indian elite alike.

Khwaja Moin-ud-din Chisti belonged to an earlier era which derived inspiration from his studies and travels to Iraq, Syria, Afghanistan and cities that spelt the magic of lost centuries — Samarkand and Bukhara. He came and settled down in India in AD 1190 and remained behind to become a part of its historical, religious and cultural memory. Gradually, over time, the tradition of singing the *qawwali* became a part of the traditional homage at his *dargah* in Ajmer, where thousands join in with eyes closed, beating time to the rhythmic beats of its devotional fervour. The content joins praise of the attributes of Mohammad with those of these two great followers of his faith.

PAGE 63
The worship that binds — at the Dargah of Khwaja Moin-ud-din Chisti

Kumbh Mela

In 1978, two million people from all corners of India and some from other countries took the holy dip at the confluence of the three sacred rivers at Prayag (Allahabad), now also known as, the famous Ganga, the Yamuna and the now subterranean Saraswati all three of which form the substance of mythological lore. A dip at their *sangam* (confluence) is considered a route to salvation and lucky are those who travel wide and are able to make it. In 1990, exactly 12 years later in the time cycle stipulated for the holy dip, the figure rose to millions of lucky or plucky ones! Though Prayag is the holiest of spots because it is the meeting point of three rivers, there are three other towns which have also earned the holy status for this 12-year cycle. They are Haridwar in the north, Ujjain in central India and Nasik in the west, all home to the Ganga, but also lucky recipients of holy nectar in a mythological story which gave them an alternate status. Here too, the Kumbh Mela or fair is held in a 12-year cycle, and all because they became incidental beneficiaries of a war between the demons and the gods!

In India, historical facts are clothed in mythology. Mythology carries the mantle of belief, and belief carries the weight of both. Perhaps, in a very fundamental sense this would be true of all nations with a teeming past and with memories carried forward through thousands of years. In addition, if you have a multi-lingual, multi-cultural, multi-geographical cauldron in which are brewed ancient memories and future hopes, you have an unbelievable diversity which can be, and is, mind-boggling. It is this diversity which is revealed in its multifarious forms at the Kumbh

Mela in Prayag. Not only do you have masses congregating in an unbelievable kaleidoscope of humanity, but you have the flag waving, insignia-holders of saintly orders in a variety that is breathtaking. Amongst these, you have even foreigners from various countries who have adopted some saintly order or the other, and are clothed in the mandatory saffron robes, even to carrying the wooden bowl as the only worldly possession. But it is the Naga *sadhus*, with their naked bodies smeared with ash which fascinates the onlookers, and are accepted with near equanimity by the vast majority who understand that it is a symbol of total renunciation. There is the belief, for instance, that when Lord Mahavira, the Jain saint, attained enlightenment, he became totally naked. That is when a white robe came wafting down the skies and slid over him. The Naga *sadhus* prefer to have ash as cover, yet it is amazing how coolly the crowd accepts this nudity as the ultimate in the renunciation of all worldly encumbrances.

The fact that three other subsidiary Kumbh *melas* are held at Haridwar, Nasik and Ujjain relates to yet another

mythological legend. There was apparently an unending fight between the gods and demons, which is really only another way of saying between good and evil, and nobody could win over the other. On discovering that a pitcher or *kumbh* which lay at the bottom of the ocean contained nectar and a sip of which ensured immortality, another fight took place when the pitcher was snatched away by God Indra's son to give to his father, with the demons running in pursuit. The drops, which fell from the pitcher during the flight at Prayag, Haridwar, Nasik and Ujjain, gave these towns the sanctity to hold the *Kumbh Mela* (Fair of the Pitcher). The *melas* do not involve only a gathering of believers. You must take a dip in the holy waters. Prayag holds the ultimate promise because it is the town at the holy confluence of three venerated rivers, and above all, where the River Ganga flows.

Maha Shivaratri

Of the Divine Trinity of Hindu gods — Brahma, Vishnu and Shiva, symbolising respectively the origin, the preservation, and death and renewal of life, it is the dynamic dancing God, Shiva, who stands for the last most dramatic aspect of the human being's journey. This, according to Hindu belief, traverses through the past, present and future till you are no longer reborn and become one with the Infinite. This is therefore symbolised by the most dramatic manifestation that Shiva can assume in his role as one who represents the dynamics of life, death, and life again. Shiva is therefore both fearful and majestic, invoking awe on the one hand, offering consolation on the other, and finally promising a tryst with infinity. No wonder, therefore, that he is in one sense, the God of all gods, and in his diverse forms, therefore also, the Lord of all the Arts. It is Shiva's dance of eternity, which is held out as the penultimate form therefore and makes him the iconic symbol for the art world. Its thunderous rhythmic syllables are like a call to pulsating life, challenging the earth, the heaven and mankind to a furious affirmation.

In one sense though, but only in one instance he signifies the triumph of the male. That is, in competition in the cosmic dance-duet with Parvati, the Goddess of Power and Universal Energy. In a triumphant show of majestic masculinity, he lifts one leg to a straight perpendicular height, and Parvati falls shy of matching that pose for the exposure that it would have entailed and loses by one point. It is on Maha Shivaratri that Shiva, however, does the famous *tandav nritya*, which comprises the 10 aspects of cosmic energy, revealing the third eye or the ultimate consciousness. This

festival then really is an ode to the grandeur of the Shiva image, the awe that is inspired by his all-pervasive dominant energy; while the revelation of the *lingam* becomes also symbolic of the perpetuity of life. The image of the *lingam* therefore now stands for Shiva's cosmic celebration of life and is worshipped for itself.

Again, like most auspicious Indian festivals, Shivaratri falls in the month of February-March on the 14th night of the new moon. It is observed not so much with public fanfare as with observing a full-day fast, and personal devotion and worship at the temples, to the chants of *Om Namah Shivaya*, a repetitive invocation to Shiva. In fact, in the symbolic tradition of Hindu religious observances, it is the *lingam* or the *Shivaling* alone, which is enough to invoke a passion of devotion and ceremonial observances. The image of the God of Life and Destruction and Life again is contained in this form as a representative force which invites worship. The carved images of the *lingam* in homes or temples are therefore bathed with milk, anointed with sacred paste and worshipped to the chanting of hymns and with offering of *bael* leaves which are considered sacred. Oddly enough, though the images of Ravana, king of Lanka, are reviled, condemned and burnt in the festivities of Dussehra, it is his learning, scholarship and his being a prime devotee of Shiva, and his Shiva *tandava stotra* which gets pride of place on Shivaratri as a paen of praise. It is sung with fervour and devotion in the celebrations at home and in temples.

Celebration of Shivaratri takes place at far off corners of India as in the south at the famous Chidambaram and Kalahasteshwara temples, Khajuraho in Madhya Pradesh, and the Sri Kalashasteshwara in Kalahasti and of course, the Shiva temple at Varanasi. There can be seen a line of pilgrims reaching out for the opportunity to worship at these and other smaller temples on the occasion of Shivaratri and make their offerings of milk and auspicious *bael* leaves.

LEFT
A tryst with the God of all gods — Shiva

Mahavir Jayanti

As the sun rises in the east, so it seems did the origins of the six main religions of the world — Hinduism, Buddhism and Jainism from India and Judaism, Christianity and Islam from the Middle East with its epicentre in Jerusalem. Even the almanac of social truisms defined as good and bad by Confucius originated in China in the Far East as did Shintoism in Japan. Though the Jain religion in India had 23 *Tirthankaras* or Prophets till 599 BC, it was the birth of the 24th, Mahavira, and his emphasis on peace and social reform that made him the symbol of Jain belief. He was a contemporary of Gautama Buddha and like him, a prince by birth. And like him too, he renounced his life of luxury. Thereafter he took his own path to spread the message of righteous conduct, involving abhorrence of violence and simplification of the religious rituals.

Though Mahavira took his inspiration from the Sramana tradition which is intertwined with the Vedic and Upanishadic, he created his own body of emphasis — his teachings were described as Nirgrantha Dharma, that is, truth lies in the entire universe and not only in one scripture. And, as he is supposed to have said, "He who knows his doubts knows the world", some of the main principles of this faith are equality between the sexes; belief in self-restraint and social discipline and in the existence of the soul; the responsibility for one's own actions and the principle of re-birth. The belief in non-violence is related to all aspects of life, hence adherence to vegetarianism and a basic kindness towards all forms of life. Lord Mahavira defined his belief in simple terms — that human beings are their own salvation, that it is

PAGE 73
*Mahavira — right
faith, right
knowledge, right
conduct*

ABOVE
*Compassion for all
living creatures*

through the three jewels that an individual can find the ultimate satisfaction and attain merit — right faith, right knowledge and right conduct.

The celebration of the birthday of Lord Mahavira in April every year becomes an occasion for emphasising these three jewels of belief in homes where families get together to reiterate their vows to vegetarianism, as an expression of compassion for the *jiva-daya*, living creatures, the recognition of universal interdependence and belief in the many manifestations of reality. Together they lead the Jains to a give-and-take philosophy which cuts at the very root of religious rigidity. It is perhaps to emphasise this that the birthday of Lord Mahavira is celebrated but also because it is the day of universal forgiveness which enjoins upon one and all: "I beg forgiveness of all living creatures as I forgive them all. I have friendship for one and all and have no ill feeling or animosity for anyone."

It is no wonder that on Lord Mahavira's birthday which falls before the onset of summer, celebrations are very austere and private. The *paryushan parva* enjoins fasting for eight days, culminating in the birthday as a day of forgiveness for all, and asking for forgiveness from all. The Khanakvashi sect among the Jains does not believe in going to temples, or in image worship. Those who go to the temples meet each other, exchange views on principals of *ahimsa* (non-violence) and do not in any way subscribe to any form of joyous celebration.

But the Indian's passion for colour, celebration and the inherent desire to share with one another cuts through Jain rectitude. Chariot processions holding the image of Mahavira roll along milling crowds towards Jain shrines at Girnar and Palitana in Gujarat and at Mahavirji in Rajasthan. The Vaishali *mahotsav* is held at his birthplace, the temples hold rich ceremonies and, though all this alternates with fasts and charities, large fairs spring up to house the overflowing enthusiasm of Jain followers. There is an interesting legend about the Lord Mahavira's enlightenment. His mother, Queen Trisala, had a series of dreams foretelling the birth of Vardhaman, her son as the 24th *Tirthankara*. The Ashoka tree became the canopy under which Vardhaman attained enlightenment after-two-and-a-half days of meditation. Thereafter, as Mahavira, he stripped himself of all worldly attachments, even his clothes. The sky-clad sect among the Jains is called the Digambara and the white-clad, Shvetambara. The Shvetambaras believe that Indra then presented him a white robe, which they too wear to identify themselves with their Master.

Navroze

Originating in Iran, Prophet Zoroaster's religious tenets travelled to India with the clan which has come to be known as Parsis, as of Persia. Settled in India since 1,000 years ago, the Parsis came when Persia was still known as Persia, while those called Persians came in only about 300 years ago when Persia reverted to its original name, Iran. Over the years, the Parsis have adapted themselves so much to the Indian cultural habitat that their origin, like that of so many who came from far off lands as travellers to settle down or even as conquerors to stay back and be assimilated into the mainstream, has became irrelevant to the primacy of being Indian. Cultured, full of life, but being a minority, they celebrate their identity with even greater zest. The fact that the Parsis divide the year into six seasons, each to be celebrated as a festival, means that there are unending feasts of joy and celebration for them. Their six festivals are called Gahambars and as with any community, they begin by celebrating the different stages of agriculture. It was only later that they began to relate to some religious happening or the other.

But it is the Parsi festival of Navroze that is the most significant. Navroze signifies two things. *Nav* means 'new' and *roze* means 'day'. It denotes spring, the birth of awareness in one's life. Secondly, it relates to the day of the equinox, when night and day, light and darkness, stand together in equal balance. So Navroze began to be celebrated as the first day of the Zoroastrian New Year and the day when Shah Jamshed chose to ascend to the throne and establish the Peshadian dynasty 3,000 years ago. It was that particular day which also began to be termed Jamshed Navroze.

It is celebrated with feasting for a new awareness of the miracle of life, when Nature assumes the vibrant mantle of spring.

The birth anniversary of their Prophet, Zoroaster falls on the 6th day of the Zoroastrian calendar, meaning the middle of the second millennium BC. It is called Khordad Sol. His followers were enjoined to a struggle for good against evil with *humanta* (good thoughts), *hukta* (good words) and *harvarsha* (good deeds). They believe that the Sacred Fire was brought from heaven by the Prophet himself, so they conduct their worship at fire temples where the fire is kept burning constantly.

The celebration of every event, however, takes place predominantly in homes in almost a never-ending delight in feasting. There is not so much dance or music in a Parsi celebration as delectable varieties of dishes for each occasion. They consist of a blend of West Asian and Indian food, beginning with *ravo*, made of *suji*, milk and sugar and fried vermicelli in sugar syrup, raisins and almonds. Following this, they offer sandalwood to the Holy Fire at their temple. Back home or with friends, it is a gastronomic celebration again. No Parsi is a vegetarian, so there are special dishes like fish in green *masala*, chicken curry, *pulao* with nuts and saffron and for every visiting guest a glass of *faluda*, chilled vermicelli, sprinkled with rose essence. Probably the most marked influence of their Indian connection is the mandatory inclusion of plain rice and *moong ki dal* as part of their culinary feast! Like many other Indian communities, the Parsis too decorate their doorsteps and entrances to homes with powdered designs and greet their guests with a sprinkling of rosewater and application of *kumkum* (red powder) on their foreheads as a greeting. But the essence of a Parsi celebration of any festival is the injunction to give to the poor and the needy a vibrant sense of equality amongst all classes when it comes to sharing the joy of welcoming another year, another '*Saal Mubarak*'.

PAGE 77
The joy of traditions

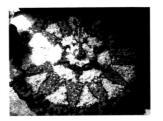

Onam

This is one of the most secular Indian festivals ever. Though Hindu in its origin, reference and mythological belief, it is so strongly associated with the seasonal reaping of the harvest and the consequent full granaries that it draws both Christians and Muslims into a celebratory participation. August-September or what is called *Bhadon* is the time of spring and Kerala particularly converts it into a festival of flowers, the speciality being the white *thumpa* flower. So the threshold of every family house is bedecked with floral designs while the Hindu households make use of symbolic earthen mounds of the Hindu God, Vishnu, and the hero of this festival, the *asura* or demon king, Mahabali. Like most festivals in India, even though the style of celebration pertains to the season, the origin goes back in time to a mythological event which has been bequeathed down the centuries in the form of a story, a myth or historic innuendo. This has been done, above all, mostly through the oral tradition. Same is the case with Onam. Though the celebrations have a seasonal impetus, the backdrop is a throwback to cultural inheritance which seems to have braved the centuries.

The Keralites are sentimental about King Mahabali who is outside the pale of the Hindu Trinity of Brahma, Vishnu and Mahadev. He was an *asura,* a demon, of lower caste, but so loved by the people for his justice and fair play that his rule extended beyond the earth to the heaven, and even to the nether world. The gods became nervous about their territorial rights and jealous of him. So the great Vishnu, in the garb of a dwarf, Vamana, approached the king to ask for the boon of land which he could cover only in three steps. The king gladly agreed. But soon, the dwarf began to grow bigger and bigger, and in one huge step, he covered the entire heaven. With the second, he strode across the nether world. Afraid that the earth would be crushed under the giant foot, King Mahabali offered his head, and was thus pushed down into oblivion. But he was held in such a high esteem by the people that the gods made a concession. He was allowed to come up once every year to be with, seen and celebrated, by his *praja*, the people. Onam commemorates the event. And so enthusiastic are the people about paying homage to his memory that the festivities begin for full 10 days before in anticipation.

What draws almost every community to such consistent celebrations are the various sporting forms that these festivities take. They relate, of course, to the verdant landscape of Kerala — its hills, dales, streams, the full breeze and swaying trees and the rains that paint everything a glowing green. Flowers bedeck the entrances to homes; caparisoned elephants parade the streets in one town, fireworks sparkle in another; the village green turns into a theatre for actors in their resplendent costumes, recreating legends. However it is the painted tigers, actors beneath the yellow stripes, green eyes, stark reds and blacks for whom the populace comes in droves to see and applaud, while instruments like *uduku* and *thakil* beat time.

Finally it is the boat race, the *vallamkali,* which is the epicentre of all celebrations. A hundred oarsmen row their *odee* (boats) to vociferous cries from the shores, and to the rhythm of drums and cymbals that beat with the dip and flow of the oars to set the pace. The boat race is a particular feature in Aranmulai and Kottayam, and the excitement far surpasses the famous boat race competition between Oxford and Cambridge!

Oddly enough, like the cultural adjustments which are so typical of India, Onam celebrates the once-a-year visit of their beloved King Mahabali with an added zest after the setting up of a temple in praise of Vamana, in the 8th century AD! Thus along with his adulation of Mahabali, the

RIGHT
A symphony in white —the thumba *flower heralding spring*

worshipper is not robbed of his other loyalties! A copper plate inscription dates the celebration of Onam to AD 861, though historical conjecture takes it even further back in history. Further the ideal of what a ruler should really be like is captured in a folk song, which could be as relevant today as it was then. It has been translated by K.K.C. Nair into English as an ode to the qualities of Mahabali:

When Mahabali ruled the land,
everyone was equal.
Happily they lived.
danger befell none.
There was no falsehood, or fraud
and no untruth, only
Equality, security and truth.

The three tenets of good governance spelt out so colourfully then are the key to what the future should hold!

Pushkar Mela

The idea of a religious fair in India is only a little different from a religious festival which, by and large, is confined to a religion or a religious sect. The town of Pushkar, only a short distance away from Ajmer in the north-western state of Rajsthan, has become a popular destination for two kinds of visitors: one, for the Hindus it is, yet again, a place for holy pilgrimage, and two, for tourists from all corners of the world who come to see its famous cattle fair, partake of the revelry that surrounds the event, and then, feel with the devotion that makes millions of believers go there every year to relive its ancient devotional lore. In recent years, Pushkar has become a particularly fascinating destination for foreign tourists because of the liveliness, the frenzy, the colour that is ingrained in the legends and topography of Rajasthan. Pushkar is so haloed a religious place for the Hindus that it draws devotees from all corners of India; and with each devotee or group of devotees comes an individual code of beliefs, dress and style that could entrance anyone — from the French fashion designer to a rural innocent from Bihar. Pushkar seems to have become really the international hub for those curious about the cult of the ash-smeared naked *sadhus* or religious mendicants who have forsaken all, or for those who want to see India in its most intriguing religious colours.

For behind the obvious rivalries of colour, pageantry and ritual, there is the origin of Pushkar. There are four acknowledged centres of Hindu belief; Badrinath, Puri, Rameshwaram and Dwarka. Pushkar, it is said, is the fifth. If you have not taken the mandatory bath in Pushkar's famed lake, you will not be able to visit the four other

places mandated by religious belief. There is as usual a mythological-cum-legend-cum-historical hint with reference to the *Padama Purana,* about how the great Brahma himself performed a *yajna* at Pushkar, hence its halloed air. But the *yajna* has, as usual, a symbolical-cum-mythological legend woven around it. And, as usual, with India's multifarious history, and its 5,000 years of past, one does not know where legend ends and history begins or where legend takes over and where history gets lost in time.

For instance, there are three temples which do actually exist in Pushkar. These are dedicated to God Brahma himself, to Savitri, his wife and to Gayatri. According to the *Padma Purana* again, as quoted by scholar and historian, Dr B. N. Sharma, when Lord Brahma decided to perform the *yajna* on *Kartika Purnima* and invited all sages, savants and gods, his wife did not turn up in time — it seems times do not change that much — and, as practical that our gods were and the ceremonial necessity for a wife very mandatory, Brahma married a Gujar girl, Gayatri, right on the spot. And lo and behold, a bedecked and bejewelled Savitri appeared on the scene and on seeing what had happened, cursed the whole congregation. As a way out then, the

LEFT
From the mists of the past — the Kumbh connection

Fairs & Festivals **85**

harassed Brahma created Shap-Mohini, on seeing whom the curse would be lifted. But in practical terms, the circumstances led to the creation of three temples in Pushkar, which are now hallowed spots. Two temples, dedicated to Savitri and Gayatri, rest above a hill-top below which is a lake. It has 52 steps down which people descend to take a dip in the belief that this would wash them of their sins.

With devotion allied to one of the most picturesque landscapes of Rajasthan and with legend giving fairytale resonance to religious belief, and as a tourist centre which draws more and more visitors to it every year, Pushkar has become a most favoured town for those who want to sample India's tryst with the past.

ABOVE
From the past — a fairytale resonance

Raksha Bandhan

The last of the first 15 days of the moon, from its full, circular glory to its tryst with darkness is called the night of *Amavasya*. This constitutes the period of *Krishna Paksha*, according to the Hindu calendar. The second fortnight, beginning with the teasing crescent of light and ending with *Purnima/Purinmashi* when the moon again attains the height of its passionate luminescence is called *Shukla Paksha*. Most of the Indian festivals relate to the ebb and flow of the moon, the sun and rain, or to incidents from mythological lore.

One such festival is Raksha Bandhan, which, like Bhai Duj, commemorates the relationship of brother and sister and draws its moral sanction from stories embedded in historical memory. There are two versions. Both relate to God Indra and his confrontation with the demons who drove him out of his kingdom and threatened to bring to end the rule of Divine law. Before Indra's teacher, the great Vrihaspati, could give him any advice, it was Indrani, Indra's wife, who promised a solution. It was the month of *Shravan*. The next day, as the effulgence of the full moon lit up the night, Indrani had a sacred thread tied to Indra's wrist before his battle with the demons. Of course, he won, and the victory was attributed to that magical thread. In another version, Indra's consort Sachi asked Lord Vishnu for help and it was he who gave her an amulet to tie on Indra's wrist to ensure his victory.

Over the years, the tying of the sacred thread has become an emotional ritual between brother and sister; the ensuring of victory has changed to the ensuring of love and protection by the brother for his sister and the hope of success, health and well-being by the sister for her brother. The sacred amulet is now a sacred red thread, but has acquired different elaborations in decoration. The one time assurance for victory is now the insurance of love and the tie is not tested in war between gods and demons but in a relationship. The ceremony is also therefore warm and a part of family ritual.

For some reason, Raksha Bandhan is celebrated more in the North and in the north-western parts if India. After an early bath, the sister is ready to take the *rakhi* to her brother in a ceremonial *thaal* or tray, replete with delectable sweets, covered by red cloth over which is placed the *rakhi*. She then sits in front of her brother, puts the vermillion mark on his forehead and fills his mouth with sweets to the laughter and singing of the elders and children filling the air. The brother in turn gives her a gift, usually cash, as a symbol of his assurance for a protected future. The *rakhi* now travels across oceans and skies and no matter where the brother is, the sister reaches out to him with this sacred thread by air or by post. So sanctified is this ritual that even if any girl, unrelated to the man, ties the *rakhi* on his wrist, he is honour-bound to offer his protection thenceforth. One of the most famous examples cited is that of King Porus from India and his famous confrontation with the Greek conqueror, Alexander. The story goes that before the impending battle, a Greek princess came to his court, tied the *rakhi* on him, and extracted the promise that he would not harm Alexander. When in the heat of the battle, Porus got ready to strike at Alexander, he remembered his promise to his sister and lowered his hand, with the result that all history knows! Another example, more recent, is of Moghul Emperor Humayun and the queen of Mewar. The queen's kingdom was laid under siege by the marauding Governor, Bahadur Shah. An agitated queen sent a *rakhi* to Emperor Humayun as a call for help. He tied the *rakhi* and then felt honour-bound to protect her. He rushed his army to the rescue of the queen and had the Governor thrown out!

The celebration of Raksha Bandhan is confined not only to private

homes but spills out to markets, ablaze with *rakhis* in innovative designs and with mouth-watering sweets in multi-hued varieties. However it is sentiments that rule the day.

Another festival celebrating the promise of a bond between a brother and sister is Bhai Duj where *bhai* means 'brother' and *duj*, denotes the 'second day' after the new moon and the third day after the grand festival of lights, Diwali. Like all Indian festivals, this occasion also draws inspiration from mythological lore. After Lord Krishna vanquished the demon Narakasur, he went to his sister Subhadra who welcomed him and as a thanksgiving, she promised to give him protection. In a different context, when Mahavira, the founder of Jainism, attained *nirvana*, his brother, Raja Nandivardhan felt bereft. It was their sister, Sudarshana, who then comforted him and became the symbol of protection and care.

ABOVE
*Tying the thread —
a foreverness of love*

In the North, the sister applies the *tikka*, the red vermilion mark made of sandal paste and *kumkum* (red turmeric), on her brother's forehead. In Maharashtra, she waves the ceremonial *thali* or tray filled with sandalwood paste, red vermilion, a few grains of rice and sweets, in a circular motion in front of her brother. She then applies the *tikka* of red powder and sandalwood paste with rice grains on his forehead. The sister decorates the floor with *rangoli*, patterns made with coloured powder. In the South, the third day of Pongal is celebrated as Kanu Pongal, when the girls in the family knead cooked rice balls in colour and place them out in the open for the crows to feast upon. With each ball that the girls knead, they offer a prayer for their brothers' well-being while the brothers give them *ponga padi* which is normally in cash form.

Rath Yatra

Every festival celebrated in India, even in the folk tradition, is woven round some mythological story which has been handed down the ages through word of mouth, from generation to generation, in village after village. If anything binds India into one, with its vast range of official and non-official languages, dialects and religions, it is its mythological treasure-trove of stories and anecdotes. This has become so embedded in the subconscious culture of the land that they tend to become almost like reference points in defining what is wrong, what is right, what is good and what is bad. There is so much rooted in so many lost centuries, that the culture carries with it a load of primeval memories.

The Jagannath temple at Puri in Orissa embodies this merging of the past with the present in all the stories that abound about the origin of the statue of Lord Jagannath. But the festival in which devotees pull three massive chariots with the idols of Jagannath, his brother Balabhadra and sister Subhadra, over 3 kilometres followed by, now over the years, a gathering of half a million devotees, has become the festival of all festivals! It is held in the months of June-July, again in relation to the Indian calendar in the lunar fortnight, on the second day. The deities are rested for 15 days at *gundicha ghara*, and then returned back to the temple. So everywhere in Orissa where the festival takes place on a smaller scale, the place where they are placed for 15 days is also called *gundicha ghara*. In modern parlance, it has begun to be called the 'car *yatra*'!

The antecedents of this festival to commemorate the placing of Lord Jagannath in the temple at Puri go back to at least 1,000 years. And again it is the all-embracing God Vishnu who plays with his many manifestations. It makes a lovely, intriguing story. King Indradyumna had a premonition that the presence of God Vishnu lay embedded in a hidden statue somewhere. He wanted that statue, and in anticipation, it was he who built the great Jagannath temple, now such a well-known pilgrim centre. But the temple kept lying in wait for the idol. It was one of the four scholars that the king sent to far off corners, the young Vidyapati, who followed his father-in-law to a hidden cave, found the statue and took it to the king. It was small. The great Vishwakarma, master craftsman in disguise, promised to make a bigger one, but in wood. On being disturbed against his instructions, he left it incomplete. So it has come to rest in Puri as the cynosure of all eyes — in its incomplete form but the object of never-ending devotion. It is one of the rarest examples in Indian architecture of an idol in wood.

So fervent was the devotion that people even believed, according to an account by Manoj Das, that they would achieve *moksha* or eternity if they got crushed under the 16 wheels of the Jagannath chariot! Like most religious festivals, there are anecdotes galore and stories symbolic of the narrative richness of Indian mythology — where truth and fiction, fact and interpretation, romance and theology, play hide and seek with historical facts and mythological references. Despite the change in the nomenclature of the *rath* or old-time chariot, the 'car *yatra*' in modern parlance of the Jagannath phenomenon continues to live and celebrate its hidden truths. In the last ritual of the Rath Yatra celebrations, the temple inside resounds to the verses of Jayadev's literary masterpiece, the *Geet Govinda*. Manoj Das has gone to extensive lengths to paint the drama of this happening and in writing about the 10 incarnations of Vishnu mentioned by Jayadev, J. P. Das, the well-known poet, translates Jayadev's verse about the last one, Kalki, who is supposed to be the *avatar* of the future:

RIGHT
The 'car yatra' —
celebrating hidden
truths

O, Hari, you carried the sword, like
a terrible comet to kill the
barbarians on Earth.
O, Keshava, you took the form of Kalki,
O, Lord of the Universe, let there be
victory unto you.

In the context of the creation of the perfect man, as Manoj Das writes, "Perhaps the present 'incomplete' form of Jagannath awaits fulfilment in the consciousness of the man of tomorrow."

ABOVE
Sacred offerings

Teej

This is perhaps the only one of three festivals that relates basically only to women. One is Karva Chauth which women in North India observe for the well-being of their husbands every year on the fourth day of the new moon. The other is *Aghoyi Ashtami*, four day later, for which only son-bearing women observe a fast for the welfare of their sons. The women who have only daughters are not enjoined to do so! The third festival is Teej, which constitutes celebration by women, as pure freedom. This is observed on the third day of the new moon. It is called Shravan Teej which falls in the month of August or Hariyali Teej, which denotes the lush greenery that characterises the season. This is when married women return to their parents' home for a brief holiday from domestic responsibilities of their own home or of their in-laws.

The festival in Rajasthan is specially celebrated in honour of Goddess Parvati. A dominant feature is, one, the freedom with which women celebrate the return to their parental home and two, the freedom from responsibility that it enjoins. The religious ritual is very much a part of the celebrations: first, the worship of Goddess Parvati at home and second, the participation in village ceremonies when the image of Parvati is taken out in a palanquin in a procession. The women come out in all their finery, singing songs in praise of the goddess and the procession, particularly in Jaipur, even consists of elephants, camels and dancers. In fact, it is all joy and abandon in the air. The story goes that the origin of the festival lies in the

homecoming of the original inhabitants displaced by conquering hordes from their beloved *bapota,* the land of their fathers.

But over the years, this return has come to signify the married daughter's first homecoming. In fact, on the first Teej festival, the boy's family sends sweets, clothes and other decorative items to the home of the bride, and along with that, a swing, or *jhoola,* which apparently stands as a symbol of joy. The girl's parents send in return as much money as they deem fit.

In Bundelkhand, in Madhya Pradesh, the festival is celebrated by creating the *hindola* or *palna,* rocking cradle, in which is housed the image of God, and which is taken in a procession through the village. Music, of course, is always a must and it is the season for singing *kajri,* which is sung in rapturous refrain.

The swing signifies, particularly in rural areas, the sense of freedom. A girl on a swing is not only a traditional motif of old paintings but a symbol of abandon, which inspires a range of poetic images in various dialects.

A folk song in particular has a most sensuous imagery and catches not only the mood of the season, but also the romanticism of freedom that the swing signifies:

> *Inki naram kalaeeyan kabhoon*
> *lachak loom letein hain*
> *Aur patak bhoom pe deti kab hoon*
> *chatak choom letein hain*

> (See how their eyelids flutter with the moves of the swing
> and how they image the colours of a myriad springs.
> See how the fragile wrists of these maidens turn the swings
> and with one quick twist, let their hands kiss the earth.)

And all, to the refrain of freedom from and yet, nostalgia for the beloved.

LEFT
Together — the challenge of balance

Tribal Fairs of Madhya Pradesh

Madhya Pradesh lies in the heart of India, *madhya* meaning 'centre' and *pradesh*, the Hindi word for 'state'. It encapsulates in a sense the cultural heart of India, with its indigenous population which comprises the ancient tribes. Here is also a treasure-house of old temples and historic sculptures both of which are combined in its famed 12th-century temple of Khajuraho where, in the typical Hindu tradition, erotic passion is shown only as a stage in life's progression towards the ultimate spiritual enlightenment. Though the usual Indian festivals are celebrated in this state as they are in the rest of India, the tribal population of Bhils and Gonds have their own special occasions for festivities and style of celebration!

Rain of Stones

In the district called Chindwara, a festival takes place on the first day of the new moon every year on the banks of River Jaam. It constitutes a throwback to the past rivalries between two clans from the village Pandurana on one side and Sawargaon on the other. It is considered to be one of the most fearful expressions of rivalry ever to be seen, and all in the name of a past era ruled by the kingdom of the Bhonsles over an area comprising a majority of the Gond tribe. The Bhonsles installed Dalpat Shah as king of the area but he soon rebelled and began to rule in his own right. It is then that the Bhonsles organised a war to be waged against him from the area called Sawargaon, but which soon enough came under the control of Dalpat Shah.

The festival evokes rivalry in the name of the residents of Pandurana on one side and Savargaon on the other. Living in amicable camaraderie throughout the year, on the occasion of the festival, the old rivalry takes on an amazingly violent form. First, the two groups from both the villages get together to offer worship at the feet of Goddess Chandi whom they all believe in. While crowds gather from early morning to watch this rivalry, the two groups then converge on their side of the river. The battle has to be fought over the symbolic trophy of a pole with a flag which stands rooted in the middle of the river and which has to be carried off by the winning tribe. But what the 'soldiers' from each group have to brave is not bullets, but a rain of stones from either side. While the crowds cheer each hail of stones as they hit those in the water, the blood from wounds add colour to the river. The stones sometimes can be like fair-sized boulders. No one dies but some wounds are deep and bloody and find succour only by applying the sacred ash at Goddess Chandi's temple at the end of the battle. The winner is always from the village Pandurana as symbolic of righting an ancient wrong. As the boy who runs away with the pole of victory when it is finally pulled out of the river-

bed, the 'soldiers' of Pandurana escort him towards the temple. They are then joined by the other warring team in a spirit of great camaraderie. Together they carry the pole to the temple and apply the divine ash which soon cures their wounds. And all the while, there is wild cheering from the spectators who gather from all parts, not only of Madhya Pradesh, but from wherever they hear of this fearful *mela* in which blood flows with impunity but sportsmanship wins the day.

Bhagoria Festival

The Bhagoria festival of the Bhil tribe in the area of Jhabua has become the most famous. It is celebrated a week after the festival of Holi; it commemorates the festive season of spring and celebrates a good harvest, but it is in the setting up of a central *haat* from where all the activities flow that its real heart lies. Again, it seeks to right an ancient wrong and commemorates a new awareness. It revolves round the concept of lost tribal kingdoms whose descendants are now seeking to re-affirm their identity. The ancient capital of the Bhil tribe was Bhagore. A weekly bazaar is now held and is called the *Bhagoriya Haat*, where young girls and boys from the Bhil tribe bring their wares, including goats and chickens, for sale and in turn buy decorative materials and make-up to celebrate the coming festivals. It is here that the free mixing of girls and boys takes on a romantic fervour and the *haat* becomes the approval ground for lasting bonds. Dancing and singing and all the joyous activity of a festival lead to a strengthening of romantic bonds or the beginning of new ones. Sometimes, the couple does not wait for any approval and an 'abduction' (with the connivance of the girl) takes place. This is later sought to be legalised and approved by the elders. Basically, the festival emphasises the freedom of choice that the tribes allow their girls and boys and which is as contemporary a tradition as can be. There is so much dancing, singing and a sense of freedom in the air that it gives the question of choice a sacred approval.

PAGE 99
In typical masculine
finery

Vishu

Of all the festivals included in India's calendar of commemoration, there is one in Kerala which concentrates purely on the benefits of Nature. No gods or goddesses are here to get you into a spiritual mode. No stories from religious texts instruct you in the morals of pious behaviour. No origins in mythological lore direct you from the here and now of earthy well-being; instead, it is love and involvement within the family, an interchange between the here and now of existence, and the sheer joy of being part of a world of Nature.

Vishu is the New Year of Kerala. It begins by seeing only that object which is considered lucky and auspicious. And it is the oldest member of the household who either takes the object around for children and other elders to see, or it is placed at a vantage point where, on waking, the members of the household are led blindfolded so that when they open their eyes on the New Year, the first thing they see is the *vishukani,* the lucky emblem. This is prepared beforehand. It consists of raw rice put inside the *urule,* a vessel made of bell metal. Over it is placed a clean, washed cloth. On either side, two halves of a coconut are filled with oil and two wicks light up the corner. What glitter over the white cloth of the *uruli* are gold coins, yellow *konna* tree flowers, a metal mirror, betel leaves and nuts, an old book of palm leaves and oddly enough, a golden-coloured cucumber!

After this, it is one celebratory merry-go-round of eating, drinking, dancing and enjoying the fact of being. The *kani* as it is called is taken even for the household cattle to see! After this, it is a joyous time for the kids. It starts with *kaineetom,* the giving of silver coins by the elders to a younger member along with a *konna* flower. This sets off a pattern of giving and receiving which acquires its own momentum of joyful sharing, even with the servants. The *sadya* or feast is mandatory of course with the celebration, particularly as it happens to be the day of the New Year. So it is the task of the women to prepare the dishes of mangoes, jackfruits, pumpkins, coconuts, and seasonal vegetables, after which the children make the rounds collecting money for the firecrackers. The older ones go round as a group to collect money for the evening celebrations, dressed up in masks covering their faces and a *chozhi* of dried banana leaves tied as a skirt. The evening fair, the Vishuwela, is a perennial attraction but there is also a stream of people which heads for the big temples like Guruvayur, Sabarimala and others.

The *chal* or *furrow* is observed in areas of Kerala where paddy cultivation starts after the monsoon, which coincides with the Kerala's New Year. Basically, however, the 14th day of April, which is actually the first day in the Malayalam month of *Medam,* is celebrated as such, hence the superstition that it must begin by seeing only auspicious objects. But there is an interesting mythological angle to the creation of Kerala and this cannot be taken out of the usual religious context. It again relates to the Almighty Vishnu in his 6th incarnation as Parashurama. He went to war with Rama in his anxiety to wipe out the entire Kshattiya caste. He realised only too late that Rama was the 7th incarnation of Vishnu. So he gave up the struggle in contrition and went into exile and meditation. The gods relented; they asked him to throw his battle-axe as far into the sea as he could, and it was from there that the land of Kerala arose!

ABOVE
Sighting the lucky emblem